Computers in Filmmaking:
Very Special Effects

01010111010100100101010100101101
0101000101011010100101101010101000

by Stephanie Wilder

Scott Foresman
is an imprint of

Glenview, Illinois • Boston, Massachusetts • Chandler, Arizona
Upper Saddle River, New Jersey

ISBN 13: 978-0-328-52513-3
ISBN 10:   0-328-52513-8

3 4 5 6 7 8 9 10 V0N4 13 12 11 10

The New Way of Filmmaking

For almost one hundred years, special effects in filmmaking changed very slowly. Movies were made using regular film. Special effects were created using camera tricks, clay models, and similar techniques.

Over the last three decades, however, special effects have changed dramatically. The introduction of computer technology has had a major impact on modern films, and it has completely changed the way many movies are made.

Most movies are still shot on regular film rather than videotape, and most moviemakers still use film cameras like the one below. But every year more and more computers are used to create special effects. In some cases, computer-based digital cameras are being used instead of film cameras.

A growing number of movies are being made with computers instead of film cameras.

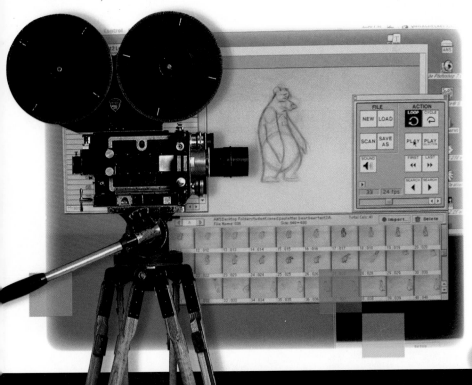

Computers:
Making the Impossible Possible

In the late 1970s, filmmakers started using computers to create movie effects. First they filmed their actors on a stage. Later they added backdrops designed by computers. This process was slow and expensive, and it wasn't capable of making realistic special effects.

In the past decade, computer technology has gotten much better. It can now create movie images that look amazingly lifelike. This is done through the use of computer pixels. Pixels are the miniature dots of color that make up the images on your computer screen.

Computer imaging has made special effects more detailed and lifelike. Today, if you want to make a movie set in a **prehistoric landscape** filled with many different dinosaurs, all you need to "create" that landscape and the dinosaurs in it is a computer.

Older movies used clay
models for special effects.

Consider what you would have needed in the past to film such a scene. You would have had to build either a huge stage or a scale model to re-create the dinosaurs' surroundings. You also would have had to make dinosaur models out of clay, rubber, or other materials. Making these models appear to move, shooting the film one frame at a time, was difficult and time-consuming.

Computer technology is a big help for re-creating past worlds, but computers can help in other ways. They can be used to cover up **background** objects. Or they can be used to add background that is too expensive to build.

Now, most movies have some computer-based special effects. Have you seen a movie recently that you're convinced was made using only regular film? Watch it again. Chances are you'll spot something that was made using a computer.

Newer movies rely more on computer-based special effects.

5

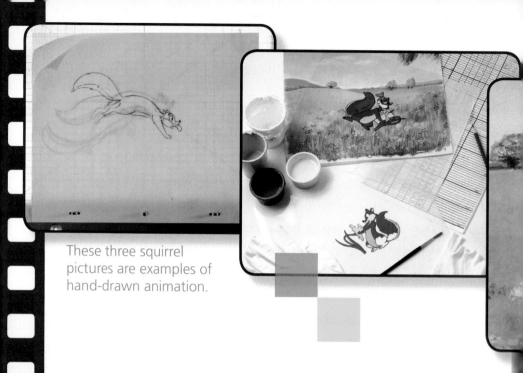

These three squirrel pictures are examples of hand-drawn animation.

Computer-Generated Characters

Perhaps the most common type of special effect is a computer-generated character. Computer-generated characters are most often created for movies that have creatures that do not exist in real life.

Early special effects used hand-drawn animation, clay models, or puppets to make these characters come to life. But today computers often are used to create these creatures. They can look more realistic than hand-drawn characters. They can be made to look three-dimensional and can be given features like fur and scales that look very lifelike. They can even blend in with live actors in a movie in a way that looks realistic.

Can you spot any differences between these computer-generated fish and the hand-drawn squirrel?

How It's Done with Computers: Preproduction

The first step in creating a scene with a computer-generated character is preproduction. In preproduction you sculpt a clay model of the character, from which you then create a computer model. The computer model allows you to see how the character will look during its scenes.

Next, using regular film, you shoot everything in the character's scenes that can't be done using a computer. This may mean filming on locations, or it may mean filming **miniature** sets of places too large to build at full size. You scan that film into a computer. When you scan film into a computer, it gets **reassembled** into a digital format. Once you have scanned the film and converted it into a digital format, you are ready for postproduction.

A computer artist uses a clay model to create a computer-based model of a dog.

A computer artist takes notes while working on three-dimensional camera tracking.

Starting Postproduction

Postproduction is where computer effects are added into the film. The most realistic way to combine digitized film and computer models is with three-dimensional camera tracking. In this process the computer artist tracks the movements of the camera used in shooting the film. The position and the angle of the camera must be determined. It would look strange if the camera that filmed the scene was pointed upward, but the computer model looked as if it were filmed by a camera pointed downward. Once the position and angle of the camera is known, the computer artist can combine live footage with computer models and make them look as if they were in the same place, being filmed at the same time.

Rotoscoping

The next step is rotoscoping. During rotoscoping, you outline the area within certain scenes. The area that gets outlined is where the character or object will be placed.

As the diagram to the right shows, there are two steps to the rotoscoping process. First the rotoscoper outlines each frame of film in which the character, or in this case the space shuttle, will appear. Twenty-four frames are needed for every second of film. That may not sound like a lot, but consider this: for the space shuttle to be onscreen for only one minute, you would need to outline more than 1,400 separate areas! Even so, rotoscoping is much faster than any similar process that uses regular film. That's because a computer can repeat many different tasks in a short period of time.

For the second step a computer artist takes each of the areas that have been outlined and blanks them out. This leaves an empty space, which the space shuttle is later added into. It sounds like difficult work, and it is. But, in a way, it is similar to any cut and paste job that you have done with scissors and paper.

The digitized film is now ready for the insertion of a computer-generated character or object, such as the space shuttle.

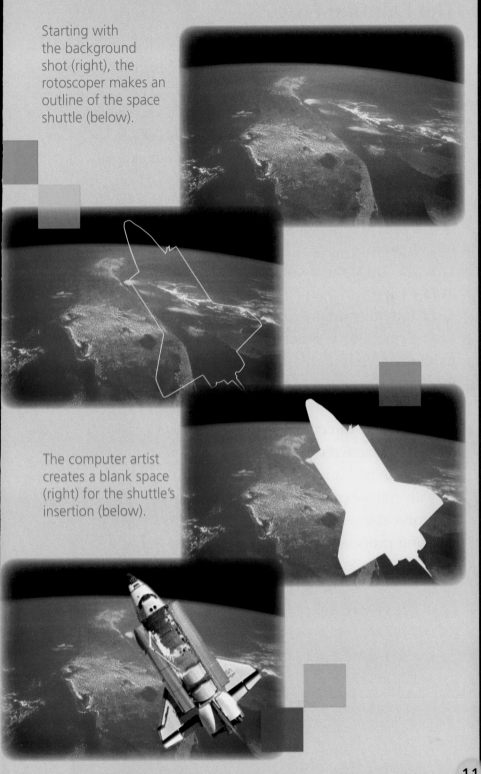

Starting with the background shot (right), the rotoscoper makes an outline of the space shuttle (below).

The computer artist creates a blank space (right) for the shuttle's insertion (below).

11

The Painting Process

The next stage of postproduction is called painting. This is when the computer-generated character is actually created!

So how is the character created? First you use a computer to create a digital model of the character, adding different features to create the character's appearance and personality. Then you insert the digitized character into the spaces that were created during rotoscoping.

To do this before computers were available, you would have had to create a separate drawing of your character for each frame. For a five-minute scene, that would have required more than seven thousand separate drawings! Instead, with computers, the character's digital model is given specific directions. These directions allow the character to be copied into each frame with much less time and effort. Just as with rotoscoping, a computer's ability to repeat the same task rapidly makes the painting process practical.

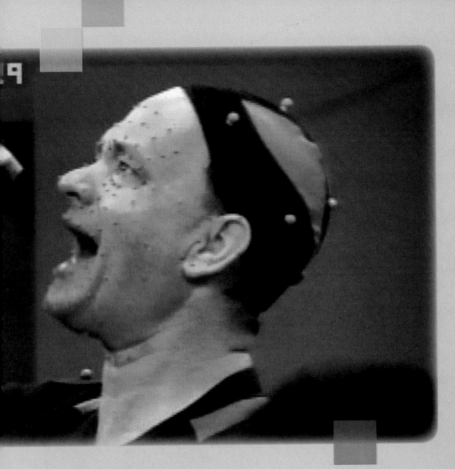

This actor's suit gives information to a computer, from which the computer creates a digital model.

Compositing

When the painting stage is finished, it is time to begin the two-dimensional compositing. During this stage, you bring together the scene's different parts.

To do this, you create many different layers. You layer the computer-generated character over the background scenes that were shot on film. In other scenes, you add in the character's friends or environment as another layer. You pile each layer on top of the other layers. When you finish piling the layers you get a whole image, complete with the movie's human actors, the computer-generated character, the background, and the special effects.

Finally, you turn the digital file, which contains everything that was done on computer, back into film. The result makes it look like the computer-generated character was filmed alongside the actors. Movies from the past used handmade puppets instead of computer-generated characters. But computer-generated characters look much more lifelike!

The digital model is combined
with the other layers of film,
thereby completing the process.

Anyone with good skills and the right computer can put together a computer-based movie!

Cell phones are now so advanced that you can make movies with them.

Comparing the Processes

Computer-generated characters are only one movie element that gets created by computers. Often, in animated features, everything is computer generated. In addition, computer-generated effects might appear in a movie that doesn't look computer generated. For example, backgrounds, explosions, or different kinds of weather may be created by a computer artist and added to a traditional film.

No matter of how much of a movie is computer generated, the final product is transferred to film before it is shown in theaters. However, today, some movies are being created in digital format and then left in digital format. These movies are not only created on computers; they are actually made to be stored and shown on computers as well. No film is involved at all.

This digital camera can also be used to make movies.

Computer-based digital movies can be edited, or made ready for release, quickly through the use of a computer. Changes can be made to any part of the movie. The computer's code simply can be rearranged to change either the order of the movie's images or the images themselves.

With regular film, the editing process requires more time and effort. The editor can only make changes by cutting out portions of the film. Then the film needs to be taped together to keep it in the right order.

So far, only a few Hollywood movies have been completely digital. This is because most movie theaters can only show movies that are on regular film. At this time theater owners don't want to buy new computer-based projectors. At present it's not worth the cost.

The following pages explore the benefits and drawbacks of entirely digital movies. After you read the two lists, see if you can come up with other advantages and disadvantages.

The man in the top photo is editing regular film. The man to the left is editing a computer-based movie.

The PROs of Computer-Based, Entirely Digital Movies

> Digital movies cost less to make. Regular film is expensive. It requires trucks and planes for distribution. With digital movies, the files can be sent directly to the movie theater over the Internet.

> Digital movies don't take up a lot of space. The only space they require is a computer hard drive!

> It's easy to make copies of digital movies.

> The editing of digital movies is easy and flexible. Changes can be made at any stage of the postproduction process.

> Digital movies don't require any film to be developed.

> Moviemakers can see immediately what they made. They don't need to wait for any film to be developed to see the day's work.

The CONs of Computer-Based, Entirely Digital Movies

> Digital movies can look grainy on a big screen. That's because they're designed to look best when played on a computer screen.

> Digital movies use a lot of computer memory. They take up a lot of space as computer files. A special digital projector is needed to show them in movie theaters.

> People can make copies of digital movies easily and can send them over the Internet. Moviemakers are worried because it's easy for people to steal their movies and copy and distribute the files of digital movies illegally.

> It would be expensive for movie theater owners to change over from regular film projectors to digital projectors. Theater owners might have to raise ticket prices to cover the cost of the new projectors.

Getting Used to Digital

Directors can make and edit digital movies for a lot less money than movies on film. But a regular film has a certain look that computer-based movies still can't quite copy. Many times, images made by computers look almost *too* perfect when they're played on a big screen. Regular film can portray shadows and characters' movements in a way that computer-based movies are still unable to show.

We're used to the look of movies made on regular film. It looks like real life. When shown using the proper technology, computer-based movies have very precise, clean images, but our minds have difficulty accepting them, both because we've seen so many images made with regular film and because it doesn't quite match what we see around us. However, digital movies are getting better every day. Because of this, many moviemakers think that digital movies will soon become more popular than regular films.

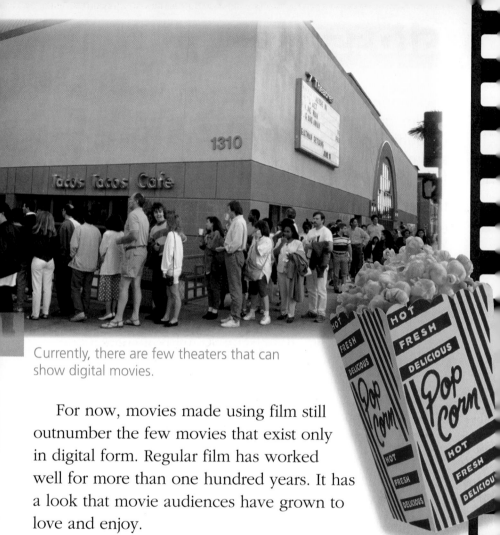

Currently, there are few theaters that can show digital movies.

For now, movies made using film still outnumber the few movies that exist only in digital form. Regular film has worked well for more than one hundred years. It has a look that movie audiences have grown to love and enjoy.

Right now, the biggest concern in the movie industry is that movies watched on a computer screen using files downloaded from the Internet will keep people from going to the theaters. It's hard to believe that people will stop going to movie theaters. But what *is* certain is that computers will continue to play a huge role in moviemaking. Special effects now rely almost completely on computers. And who knows? Perhaps some day the movies you see at theaters will exist only on computers!

Glossary

background *n.* in a movie, the images that show up behind the actors and other objects in the foreground.

landscape *n.* the look and quality of the land when viewed from far away.

miniature *adj.* the quality of being made on a very small or tiny scale.

prehistoric *adj.* from or of a time long before people began writing and keeping records and histories.

reassembled *v.* brought things back together again.